Songs from the Black Moon

SONGS FROM THE BLACK MOON

Rasu-Yong Tugen,

Baroness de Tristeombre

gnOme

ISBN-13: 978-0615969008 (gnOme books)
ISBN-10: 0615969003

Please address all inquiries to:
gnOmebooks@gmail.com

Et moi, il me semblait - tant la fièvre est incohérente! - que la lune, grimant sa face, me tirait la langue comme un pendu!

~ Aloysius Bertrand, Gaspard de la Nuit

I.

While you and I, we both sleep
and give way to all the ringing things
we do not see or hear or feel.

Solitude and silence and contempt for the world...this is my
unending prayer, desecrated with all the austerities of dried,
dusk-laden, secreted wings.

All bodies are shimmering, honeydew cadavers,
and all cadavers are powdered black onyx,
and every limb and tendon and nerve
the humility of small crepuscular plants.

There is no grace, no redemption, no reciprocity, neither
affirmation nor acceptance, nothing deserving and no
dignity, not even the unimportant or the insignificant.
There is only our failure to become impersonal, and our
indifferent devotion.

"The Rule is quite simple..." you said, almost lovingly, to me.
"Embracing nothing outside you produces an inner
tranquility, just as embracing nothing inside you produces an
outer quietude."

II.

Seeping into the pores of everyday life - there is an almost
divine malaise...

"for if I sink down
to the world,
you are still present."

III.

In the spare moments of our molecular and amethyst estrangement, I try to think up well-founded proofs and clever axioms. But what is there really to say, except that there is an abyss inside of me, a vast, breathable black abyss whose disaffection knows no bounds, whose contempt knows no bounds, whose excited dismissals know no bounds - the melodrama of it is appalling.

IV.

Disaffection, like a morass, wells up within us both, exuding
mists and mud, tossed and spilled over, deafened by the din
of our obligations and disclosures...

...this and luminescent arcs of confusion, hovering
somewhere over the low aquatic floors of brittle stars...

I was silent then,
but you were more than silent,
you were hidden -

hidden behind fragile eyes that made themselves like granite
and yet gave everything away.

V.

Where were you then, and had I been abandoned to the redoubtful, ossicle tranquility of your slow patience?

There were things unspoken I should have listened to with more care.

VI.

We have made ourselves subaqueous sand dunes, and sand dunes, you say, are the gardens of divinity, since there is not even the trace of a footprint for the wind to efface and the desert to devour.

VII.

In the hissing cauldron of noonday angst, each hour and each minute is listlessly spent among a background pantomime of attentive significance, among all the rudiments of banality, of precondition, of condescension and carelessness, of what amounts to bare activity.

Something to do, something to say, something I choose not to do, something I prefer not to say.

In some remote region there are organisms that dare not live, composed as they are of all the impassivity of stellar dust and strange geometries.

VIII.

Let me cloud over every emerging thought, and let every
task become muddied and slough off like so much dead skin.

Let black clouds of frustration engulf everything that is not
necessary, and then let it obliterate all necessity.

Let each thought that deludes itself burst forth into a
bouquet of crystalline boils and ulcerations.

Let each thought that wants to greedily raise itself up abscess
and drown with all the fungal rapidity of lush, overgrown
ruins.

In the midst of this black joy let nothing escape, except
perhaps a hesitant, hushed, badly written *De profundis* -
etched in liquid black granite in a region of remote space as
remote as you or I feel from a world deserving only of
contempt...of this joy.

IX.

We awake each morning to be inundated by myriad gestures of insignificance. All of this - the lethargy of existence, the burden of our brains, the blemish of consciousness.

We will go on enjoying our suffering on display, and enjoying our further suffering when it is not on display, all the while watching each other emote, and gesture, and watch with sunken eyes.

All the while I cower in fear, unsure if this is how one emotes, and gestures, and watches - is this how it's done?

And how is it I am still so naïve?

X.

In the listless, tepid moments of waiting to do all the things I'd rather not do, all thoughts seem to be nothing but consolation - and whatever it is that levitates windlessly above each carefully drawn circle can only come from the slow frenetic thronging of black Nymphaeas.

Often I tried to lift myself, only to plunge the deeper.

In the meantime I go on and you go on and we wallow excitedly in the moss-ridden mire of so many delusions - all other efforts that we surely should have tried, all austerities, all devout, unceasing, and earnest appeals - they themselves become nothing more than secret admonitions. We wished that our life would not be separate from a kind of prayer...

A luminescent *Book of Black Hours* blackly written with all the delicacies of whispers and murmurs, borne out of affectation and disaffection, delivered with all the hushed intonations of impersonality...

And after all this it seemed we were still left to twist and turn, in the dark.

XI.

There was never anything that made it better, never a newfound attitude of self-reliance, never any strength that was lost to be recovered, I was never in a condition to listen to what you had to say, you were never spared the farce of my opinions, we were never taken into safe-keeping for some later, imaginary consolation.

On sleepless nights my mind grows somber with grief and yet nothing had happened to cause this. My own body became a logical absurdity. My own room became an ebullient parody of life as it played itself out on some remote and sad planet.

All that we had done became a grim ordeal, my greatest fears come true in the minutiae of clinical routine. My eyes searched everywhere for some sign of something that would confirm or deny, affirm or negate, but there was nothing, only a terrifying and grandiose anonymity. I began to despise all the faces simply because of this, because they would no longer whisper to me - "no one is here!" I had become what I had always been, a riddle to myself, or a joke.

I asked predictable and pretentious questions to myself, and to my sleep, and to the void: "Why are you so downcast?" "Why are you always so distressed?" "Why have you still not learned the grand art of living in the moment?" "Why do you not enjoy what life has to offer?" But there was never any answer, and my body, with each passing day, continues to grow downwards and downcast, to laboriously pump blood and brain, to stiffen and stretch, to sigh and ache, to excrete what only a moment ago I would have vomited.

And so sighs alone have been sweet to me, since they have

taken the place of living.

And if I'm lucky the sighs will eclipse living entirely, and this is all that will remain.

But that is obviously a fantasy.

XII.

What idiocy, to think of a person as more than a person, to think of a human being as more than a human being - and what a strange pathology, to then love a human being as more than a human being. How clever we are, grumbling or rejoicing at the life we seem to accidentally live, grumbling or rejoicing, rest and agitation, the entire range of our vocabulary.

We do nothing but live accidentally, nothing but die incidentally, and only the most clever stand forth and embrace this, in a divine injunction of our own making. At last we contemplate ourselves, and in so doing we imagine we have outwitted the accident of living.

XIII.

Each of us does nothing but carry around a corpse. Our own brains are a burden, we are the asses that ache beneath its weight, slumped over our backs like thousand-pound sacks of doubtful grey matter...

Burden, bruise, and bleeding, tired of carrying it all around, and yet the curvatures of our backs have by now been perfectly molded to its heft - a burdensome brain sinking even deeper into the spine, its weight and its density made greater by the stark starfish sky and the hush of forgotten minerals and forgotten forests.

There is no peace in song or laughter, none in the company of friends or family, none in the tedious concoctions of pleasures we proudly imagine make life worth living, none even in the refusal of living, and none in the incessant, cacophonous chatter of a species so fragile and insecure, bellowing beneath the load of its gelatinous organs of self-importance.

Everything that is not the nocturnal sky, the hush of fireflies, the nameless gem-covered sea dunes, everything that is not this is dull and distasteful - just as is my sitting here now, gazing upon them all, greedily describing them and assigning attributes towards which the sky and the insects and the jewels are indifferent.

XIV.

I have patience only for the kind of sighs that are utterly lacking in experience, for it is in these alone that I find a kind of consolation (and the same can be said of tears).

And why am I embarrassed to admit this to you?

XV.

It was neither myself nor you that I believed in, but some empty figment.

It was the figment that was the problem, not the fact that it was empty.

XVI.

Is there any condition in which I am not quicksand to
myself? Even the carnivorous plants of a thousand
fingertipped moons are skeptical of all my efforts.

XVII.

A sigh of fatigue - why are we so fickle, as fickle as a breath - or winds?

XVIII.

My undying contempt for how much you know, for your
ability to describe everything, for your compulsion to explain
everything, for your elevated duty of helping and not
hindering, for your upstanding morality of "if you're not part
of the solution then you're part of the problem." I spit
venom and excremental tears upon our shared
insignificance.

And no one listens because no one can hear, and no
one can hear because it's simply too loud. Would I prefer to
doubt everything, to believe everything, to question nothing,
to do nothing, would I prefer not to be heard, not to speak,
to think? Is there anything in any utterance that is not
belligerence and disappointment? Is there any utterance that
is not really an elevated grunt or a weak falsetto cry?

We lack even the ability to derive the most adequate
insult towards ourselves. Language falters where contempt
flourishes.

Let us be reduced to the status of soil and worms and
silted matter.

XIX.

I thought it outrageous to believe that you had the shape of a human body and were limited within the dimensions of limbs and organs like our own.

XX.

For my own reasons, I fervently prayed that you and I might someday become a similar type of substance, a shapeless and hideous mass, a mass that might also be exhaled, which obscure theologians would call by obscure names like a fine and rarified stellar dust.

And once, in some old books, I read that we had exchanged imperishable limbs and organs for birds and beasts and reptiles, and that even our bowels had been woven with spools of parchment and our joints into shards of bloodless bamboo reeds, making only the faintest low whistle when we moved, like mourning doves.

XXI.

The world is far away and indifferent, colorless and flat, grey and shadowy. It is as if I am alive but do not live in the world. I see everything through a cloud or shrouded in mist. I see things, I touch things, I sit up, I walk, I talk, I sleep, but none of it comes any nearer. Other people - are they people? - slowly shift about in a furtive shadowplay, and sullen sounds seem to arrive from some distant moon. Everything is a theater, a screen, a tapestry, everything floats by and leaves no impression. I weep false tears, I keep unreal hands.

XXII.

In the dimly-lit terror of life unending you spin the whirling planets.

XXIII.

Earth invisible and without form
Darkness over the deep
Who will hear such cries
In such vastness?

XXIV.

There is a darkness that reigns over the deep -
and what is up is what is down,
and the quiet vertigo in my ears
is the slumbering turning
of diffident dripping black moons.

XXV.

Years are my sighs
and this abyss my only solace.
You are my only solace.

XXVI.

I elicit a grim, sobering farewell.
Cast off my limbs in the wild to be eaten by beasts and birds.
As it was in this life so be it also after my death.

I adhere to every melodious injunction
to be in the world but not of it.

At the end of each day
let me take account of
the most profound
and the most simple
sense of irrelevance -

producing only the lowest overtones,
and with all the studied patience of a mechanical clock.

XXVII.

I realize I should not have come along. Doubtful silhouettes
merge and emerge into and out of grotesque aquarium
scenes. I have a sense that my being here, my speaking, my
listening, even my silent thoughts, exude some kind of
dense, heavy, blackened fluid that creeps across the floor
and into the abandoned corners of the room where only the
debris of a forgotten apex has come to rest.

And so what is, you ask, the mystery of negation?

XXVIII.

I struggle with belief and you breathe in life; at the furthest limit of all hesitation I discover and rediscover the ecstatic grief of futility.

I find myself convicted of all convictions, and you, you have already tried something new. All convictions turn to indictments of what I must have already known.

I remain open to all the songs of abrogation that seem to course through my brain in the tear-laden sleep of cognition. You remain open and remain more open, infinitely open - even, and especially, open to what I most fear. You remain open to the seraphic and invertebrate dusk, to what could be or should have been, to our hermetic and deep mauve moonstone sleep. In myriad dimensions tarnished chromatic pieces of bark and branch and lichen fall upon your slender fingers and wrists and your reverberant and tranquil black hair.

I accept the intuitions of our simple finitude, and with the fervent awe of axioms I accept the futility of being what we are. You accept acceptance.

XXIX.

Even when we are close you are invisible and without form;
there is a special kind of darkness that reigns over the deep.

Even when we are entwined you are invisible and without
form; there is a black glow even in the deepest sleepwalking
seas.

Even when we have each other in our thoughts you are
invisible like our crystalline joints and our fibrous limbs and
as tangible as the shadowplay of thought itself.

XXX.

As moss and mineral creep over our furrowed hands and troubled limbs, renunciation is unearthed by our strange and impassioned austerities.

A profusion of abstract, coiling vines scream silently upwards, loosening their leaves, leaving nothing but the dizzying array of their twilight stillness.

We are mottled with unearthly growths, serene stone and graphite assemblies hidden deep in the overgrowth of our contempt for the world.

These are the last days, the worst of times,
every day the last day, every moment the worst of times.
Let us refrain from keeping watch.
Let us refuse to have so much.

And what is our inertia compared to the stillness of suspended planets?

XXXI.

After we had finished reading we left each book where it was, opened on a particular page, with some of the pages listlessly levitating, and some of them shuffling back and forth with such subtlety that makes one forget the languorous breeze, itself listlessly shuffling dust and dim light up and down the corridors, along the bookshelves, across slow breaths and slower eyelids.

The books have proceeded to turn into crystal, unfurling themselves in tiny calcifications, dotted all over like a fruiting, flowering leprosy that refracts only ambiguous colors, casting a myriad microscopic shadows across page, parchment, and leather.

The books all turned to crystal, covering the surface of each page, covering the corners of each book, constellated up and down the page edge, until the books could no longer be read, could no longer be opened or closed, until they began to shimmer in their immobility - become like cavernous rock or the dust blown off from brittle black shale.

We had read slowly or frenetically, and at the same pace at which we had written, at a pace barely a page ahead of the salt-like shimmering spreading across this book and this page and this phrase.

XXXII.

My dusk is noonday, and your crying eyes bring down all
twilight thoughts into a gulf more profound than the limbs
and tendons and muscles and organs of our sleeping bodies,
half-intentionally half-entangled.

I despise myself in myriad ways, each day anew, and there
are many things I know about you that I do not know about
myself.

I know - you know - that really we are nothing more than
the anonymity of dust and dirt and ashes; we are dimly
reflected in a dimly reflective glass, fleeting and impassive -
and we glimpse only a chiaroscuro of hair, spices, mist,
feather, fur, smiles, analogies, tendrils, and harmonies or
disharmonies.

XXXIII.

We had posed unreasonable questions to unreasonable things; we asked the tomb of the night sky, and the chasms of the calm seas, and the deep and luminous living things that creep in their luminescent depths; we asked the arid emptiness of all winds and even the dusts that settle and solemnly mock the end of each towering glass day and the start of another forest night; we asked the jagged shale rocks, and the slow cavernous stalactites, and the minerals and gems entombed in their own cavernous incertitudes; we asked the mimetic clouds, the pre-dawn mists, the undulating exposed roots and tendrils of large timeless trees. We asked the whole mass of our tectonic sorrow, the most fragile part of our bodies, the most tenuous aspect of our spectral limbs, the least reversible, the least recognizable part of ourselves - and the answer was always the same: "...and as for the other things in life, the more we weep for them the less they merit our tears, and the fewer tears we shed for them, the more we ought to weep for them..."

XXXIV.

We no longer bother to recognize ourselves. Who is to carry the research beyond this point? We are investigating the axioms of black moons, measuring the liturgy of each rotating starfish, predicting how and why our mud-laden bodies hang in heavy space, and from all this we only learn that whatever is not us is far from us, far from our grasp, and most of all far from you and I.

Through all this, I recall the health and sickness of our own bodies. The blind, stillborn inertia of my thoughts at once appalls and fascinates me.

And then you reply - we are fit to stay where we are, unwilling though we are. We want to be elsewhere, though we are not fit for it. We have a double cause for sorrow.

XXXV.

By day and by night the symphonic, sleepwalking insects cast
a vast net of delicate, pinpointed sounds across all of space.
Their numbers are exceeded only by the innumerable pin-
lighted stars that puncture the night sky, that indicate the
innumerable dead planets that long ago heaved one last tired
sigh.

And around you this night a thousand million firefly
anatomies breathe in and out in their slow-burning liturgical
glow.

XXXVI.

Even in the quiet of noonday trees, and leaves of foreboding gestures that hesitate in the quiet of the quietest breeze, even here there is the faintest hum of hermetic insects, each encased in obscurely-angled diadems - they emit hidden intonations, and we hear them only at the outer rim of our own hearing, only at the upper limit of our senses. We don't listen to them directly, since they will vanish in an acoustic hush of our busy attentiveness. Instead we listen obliquely, as if we were deaf to the sounds of this world, as if we had refused to listen to the cacophonous din of our own organism.

Even in the quiet of the most immobile, half-exposed roots there is the faint and spectral harmonics of every busy carcass, of the verdurous epiphyte dusk, almost motionlessly fanning outwards in a multitude of translucent tendrils, in long and languorous jellyfish tails that indifferently reach our ears and reach through our ears and bypass every auditory canal until we no longer hear anything, except perhaps the vaporous atmosphere itself.

And then we think of everything that we cannot hear, the hermetic insects whirling around our dim ephemeral awareness, just out of the range of our imagination - their quiet and constant humming that must cause the most subtle vibrations and the most nuanced harmonics - their nocturnal, celestial clamor that must imperceptibly shake the ground and shift large geologic rocks, and perturb the atmosphere so that the fluttering of human speech becomes a mere symptom of our own insect deafness.

Even in this tenebrous hall of mosses there is a wind-blown hush far removed from the pollution of light, distilled to nothing except our own internal nocturnal gaze, damp and disoriented.

XXXVII.

There is a somber and sorrowful stirring that drifts upwards from the polyphony of jointed, fibrous branches and slow tendrils - so slow they seem to interpret the geological time of our lunar, transported sitting.

There is a lamentation that drifts up from the seaweed depths of the night in solitary tones that sleepwalking hush forth, as our slumberous bodies crouch together and are entwined in a coral embrace.

There is a mourning owl echo, a soft and forgiving aphasia gliding outward so effortlessly that everything - you and I and the forlorn whining world about us - everything is encased in shards of prismatic black stillness, everything embalmed in the anodyne ether of quiet pure tones.

There is a sound of tranquility that is the sound of stillness, the sound of our oblivion.

XXXVIII.

We are like those huddled spirits
driven to seek the company
of the opaline seahorses
as they slowly descend to the depths.

There, we fall asleep.

XXXIX.

Days and nights when even the stars softly grumble to themselves.

XL.

Rosary of stars, seaweed skins, the once-warmed, opaque
gems of night.

Sleep descends, sleep ascends.

XLI.

Unreflective floating seaweed
drifts through your mouth and skin.

Tempests ground
about your jeweled feet.

And the artificial colors
of twilight autumn mists
begin to form your shadow.

Every triumphant moment
spreads out its wings
on our night-owl's bed.

XLII.

The architects descend into the sea,
the masons ascend into aether,
you are blessed by the alchemists and
the geometers who have departed
for the desert.

And still no one hears you.
And still no one listens to you.

XLIII.

You sleep, and your eyes like luminous black stars, your
fingers like a forest.

XLIV.

All the trees whose names we have forgotten have long since embraced our entwined limbs.

XLV.

The stars whisper into your ear: "Your swarming, sleeping, elliptical and matted hair on the pillow is the perfect expression of quiet."

XLVI.

A night-time robe of obsidian draped over our most adored,
most anonymous thoughts.

XLVII.

Across your tranquil, tenebrous forehead pass apparitions
retrieved from the dimly-lit dusts of oblivion.

XLVIII.

A languorous pause -

I watch you sing
to the subterranean, precipitous creepers
and ask them which path to take.

XLIX.

In eternal night,
we had each burned the forest
in order to better see.

Clouds of sorrowful ravens
drifted upwards,
imperceptibly blotting out the stars.

L.

These planets that turn with all the slowness of geometry.

LI.

In winter mornings,
lush, verdantique shapes
hover noiselessly
on the slightest sound.

Entire forests levitate.

LII.

Unable to recall the number of times I wish I was asleep.

LIII.

My deepest, most intimate hatred was saved for you,
every thought an ember.

But you go on doing what you do,
and I am in my dream-world.

The solace of sleep.

LIV.

To let others play their part. To observe, sullen and
confused. My willful apprehension towards your efforts.
Until the levity also becomes sullen and sad.

LV.

...the walking insomnia of each day's stirring...

LVI.

I love the sedate, anonymous movement of the overcast
clouds below, the fir and the pine trees, the geologic crags
and fissures that no one can ever see.

LVII.

If only I could persevere -
to be no more than
a dimly-lit and derelict dream.

Stillness is a lichen garden,
Solitude a kind of joy,
An inner contempt more tranquil than these nice-sounding
words.

Do not follow me.
Without a way
there is no going.
Without a life
there is no living.
Without a why
there is no knowing.

Live as a stranger on the earth.
For this earth of ours is no planet.

gnOme is a secret press specializing in the publication of anonymous, pseudepigraphical, and apocryphal works from the past, present, and future.

"Each of us is not one, but no one, not somebody, but nobody, a profusion of non-selves. So that the self who disdains its surroundings is not the same as the self who suffers or takes joy in them. None of them are anything; all of them are nothing" (Barão de Teive).

gnOme is acephalic. All profits from print sales go to the authors.

gnomebooks.wordpress.com

Other titles from gnOme

Brian O'Blivion • *Blackest Ever Hole*

Eva Clanculator • *Atheologia Germanica*

M.O.N. • *ObliviOnanisM. Volume I: Dissolving*

Pseudo-Leopardi • *Cantos for the Crestfallen*

Y. O. U. • *How to Stay in Hell: Inspiring Instructions for Daily Living*

HWORDE

Nab Saheb and Denys X. Arbaris • *Bergmetal: Oro-Emblems of the Musical Beyond*

Yuu Seki • *Serial Kitsch*

Doktor Faustroll • *An Ephemeral Exegesis on Crystalline Abrasions*